Would You Rather? Game Book

EXTREME...

RANDOMS...

WOULD YOU RATHER?

Sow up your mouth

OR

Sow up your asshole

WOULD YOU RATHER?

Hot wax in your eye

OR

Hot wax on your privates

WOULD YOU RATHER?

Give oral sex twice everyday for 1 year

OR

Give anal sex once everyday for 1 year

WOULD YOU RATHER?

Be chased by 100 duck size horses that want to fuck you

OR

1 horse size duck that wants to fuck you

WOULD YOU RATHER?

Poke your eye 3 times
with a needle

OR

Sit on a needle just once

WOULD YOU RATHER?

3 people scrap sandpaper across both of your nipples

OR

The same 3 people wipe your ass with it

WOULD YOU RATHER?

Nipple clamps

OR

Baby toe hit with a club hammer

WOULD YOU RATHER?

Be dropped inside a bottomless net in shark infested water

OR

Be dropped inside a bottomless net in crocodile infested water

WOULD YOU RATHER?

Win 100,000

OR

Your worst best friend
win 1 million

WOULD YOU RATHER?

Have No phone for a year

OR

Have no internet access
at all for a year

WOULD YOU RATHER?

Have the power of flight

OR

Have the power of invisibility

WOULD YOU RATHER?

Be in love with your wife,girlfriend, husband, boyfriend

OR

Have your secret lover win the lottery

WOULD YOU RATHER?

Kiss a donkeys butt

OR

Have a donkey kiss you after he licked his butt

WOULD YOU RATHER?

A shark bite

OR

A bite from a poisonous spider but still live

WOULD YOU RATHER?

Walk naked on broken glass

OR

Walk naked on hot coal

WOULD YOU RATHER?

Gargle a full glass of jiss
for 1 minute

OR

Gargle a glass full of the
hottest ever chilies in salt
water for 15 minutes

WOULD YOU RATHER?

Bite off one of your fingers

OR

Have your best friend bite off your big toe

WOULD YOU RATHER?

Wake up naked in a field of people you don't know

OR

Wake up naked at a surprise party with everyone you know

WOULD YOU RATHER?

Run naked 50 miles from home

OR

Run naked at your local shopping center

WOULD YOU RATHER?

Be in a dark room full of snakes for 1 hour

OR

Be in a dark room full of spiders for 2 hours

WOULD YOU RATHER?

Punch Mum in the face

OR

Punch Nan in the face

WOULD YOU RATHER?

Secret sex with partners best friend

OR

Threesome with partner and partners best friend

WOULD YOU RATHER?

Have the sexiest hottest partner ever, but no sex

OR

An ugly partner with wild kinky hottest sex ever

WOULD YOU RATHER?

Have sex with partners mum

OR

Have sex with partners dad

WOULD YOU RATHER?

Lose all taste buds for 1 year and eat only chicken soup

OR

Lick a sweaty butt hole for a hour a day for 1 year

WOULD YOU RATHER?

Anal for the first time while 6 of your best friends watch

OR

Double penetration for the first time while live on TV

WOULD YOU RATHER?

Swallow fresh sperm everyday for 1 month

OR

Give up sex for 6 month

WOULD YOU RATHER?

Save a puppy from death

OR

Save 2 really old dogs
from death

WOULD YOU RATHER?

Pull off your baby finger nail with pliers

OR

Walk barefoot in bathtub full of drawing pins

WOULD YOU RATHER?

Be buried alive in a coffin

OR

Buried to your neck in
sand at a nudest beach

WOULD YOU RATHER?

Go down and give oral on the same sex gender

OR

Get dry fucked by a super size automatic dildo that someone else has control of

WOULD YOU RATHER?

Freeze a cat

OR

Freeze a puppy

WOULD YOU RATHER?

Find £50 covered in fresh cow shit

OR

Find £100 in a fish tank with 2 giant piranha's

WOULD YOU RATHER?

Be a hot famous super star for a day

OR

Have sex with your idol for 30 minutes

WOULD YOU RATHER?

Hung by your hands at 10,000 feet up with itchy privates

OR

Hung by your privates with itchy feet

WOULD YOU RATHER?

Eat apple pie that taste like shit

OR

Eat shit that taste like apple pie

WOULD YOU RATHER?

Fuck a hot looking zombie with bloody rotten flesh

OR

Get get fucked by a hungry vampire

WOULD YOU RATHER?

Suck off a horse size dick

OR

Have a horse size dick suck you off

WOULD YOU RATHER?

Be a woman with a dick

OR

Be a man with a fanny

WOULD YOU RATHER?

Drink a cup of chicken sperm

OR

Drink a cup of your own sperm

WOULD YOU RATHER?

Suck off your partners dad

OR

Your partners dad suck you off

WOULD YOU RATHER?

Eat a 50p size bit of cats shit everyday for 1 month

OR

Eat a mouthful of zit puss everyday for 1 week

WOULD YOU RATHER?

Have sex with an ugly smelly fat person, but the sex is really really good

OR

Have sex with the hottest sexiest wildest woman you have ever seen, but she has a dick bigger than yours

WOULD YOU RATHER?

Partner walks in on you while you self love with your toys

OR

Walk in on your partner while they self love with their toys

WOULD YOU RATHER?

Sell your pride and joy car which took you years of saving to get, because your partner hates it

OR

Trade in the partner and keep the pride and joy car

WOULD YOU RATHER?

Grandad's jizz all over your face

OR

Your own jizz in your mouth

WOULD YOU RATHER?

Drink a pint of pigs piss, that makes you look 15 years younger

OR

15 years of living the same day at your hottest look ever

WOULD YOU RATHER?

Your man finds your g-spot with his tongue every time

OR

You find your mans g-spot with your tongue every time

WOULD YOU RATHER?

Lick your Nana's sweaty armpit

OR

Nana licks your sweaty armpit

WOULD YOU RATHER?

Give your dog Acid and
watch it freaking out

OR

Give your Nan acid record it
and watch her freaking out

EXTREME OF THE EXTREME

Only continue if you are not squeamish or easily offended in any way.

Remember it's a game and only a bit of fun

YOU HAVE BEEN WARNED

WOULD YOU RATHER?

Continue OR Leave

WOULD YOU RATHER?

Fuck your grandad and come all over his face

OR

Give your Nan oral until she comes all over your face

WOULD YOU RATHER?

Suck off a stallion horse

OR

Lick out a mare horse

WOULD YOU RATHER?

Your daughter be a slut and get paid well

OR

Your son be a naked dance for gay men and women and get paid pennies

WOULD YOU RATHER?

A 7" dick which last 20 minutes up your ass

OR

A 4.5" dick that last an hour up your vagina

WOULD YOU RATHER?

Have your sister bite out your tongue

OR

Bite down on a cut throat razor blade

WOULD YOU RATHER?

Bang your hot sister

OR

Get a blow job from an
ugly step sister

WOULD YOU RATHER?

Die being hot slag whore

OR

Die being a 25 year old virgin

WOULD YOU RATHER?

Lick the inside of a
dirty toilet bowl

OR

Clean your teeth with a
toothbrush that was used to
clean that toilet bowl

WOULD YOU RATHER?

Get anal fucked by a Rhinoceros horn

OR

Get a blowjob from a T-Rex

WOULD YOU RATHER?

A poisonous snake crawls up your ass

OR

Give oral to a family member of your choice

WOULD YOU RATHER?

Get hit by a fast moving bus and live

OR

Get hit by a slow moving train and live

WOULD YOU RATHER?

Blind folded to reveal you licking out your ugly half sister

OR

Blind folded to reveal you licking out your 80 year old first grade school teacher, but now she called Bob

WOULD YOU RATHER?

Blind folded to reveal you naked and strapped to mum and dads bed

OR

Blind folded to reveal you Naked and strapped to a bed out in the busiest and local shopping center

WOULD YOU RATHER?

Eat your own shit

OR

Be fed someone else's shit

WOULD YOU RATHER?

Live with a nagging talking bitch with millions but with wicked hot kinky hard core sex 6 times a day

OR

Live alone with billions but with wicked hot kinky hard core sex only once a year

WOULD YOU RATHER?

Go down on your mum everyday for a year and get I million, but everyone knows what you did to get your money

OR

Go down on your dad just once and get 10,000 but no one knows

WOULD YOU RATHER?

Fuck your sisters ugly
fat smelly best friend

OR

Go down on yourself
and swallow

WOULD YOU RATHER?

Eat your wife's or Husband's ass just as they Fart

OR

Win 10 million leave the wife/husband but smell that fart every time you open your mouth

WOULD YOU RATHER?

First time anal with 14" big black dick named Desmond

OR

Choke on your dad's dead dad's sperm

WOULD YOU RATHER?

Destroy your best friend's wedding day by telling everyone you fucked the groom

OR

Destroy your best friend's Honeymoon by turning up and fucking the bride and the groom so badly they get a divorce

WOULD YOU RATHER?

Tell the wife her ass is big and is fat with what ever she wear's

OR

Always lie, and tell her she look lovely and has a cute small ass with what ever she wear's

WOULD YOU RATHER?

Tell your wife that dress makes you look fat.

OR

Hear her say ... You have a really small dick.

WOULD YOU RATHER?

Shit your pants in the grocery store

OR

Have your kids walk in on you having sex?

WOULD YOU RATHER?

Get crabs from a hooker

OR

Be seen by a good friend at a gay bar

WOULD YOU RATHER?

Wear your friends dirty shit stained smelly underwear

OR

Drink rats piss for survival

WOULD YOU RATHER?

Donate your balls to science

OR

Donate your eyes to a blind person

WOULD YOU RATHER?

Swim in a pool of baby's green stinky shit

OR

Swim in a pool of your own piss 2 hippo's while on acid

WOULD YOU RATHER?

The wife gives you crabs and admits cheating

OR

Marry a hooker with crabs and money

WOULD YOU RATHER?

Eat puke that some one already puked up

OR

Let some one puke in your mouth

WOULD YOU RATHER?

Suck on your sister used tampon

OR

Drink a full glass of your brothers sperm

WOULD YOU RATHER?

Dig out your eye with a fork

OR

Dig out your eye with a spoon

WOULD YOU RATHER?

Get fucked by a ghost
you don't believe in

OR

Have to power to see real ghost

WOULD YOU RATHER?

Find your grand parents staring and fucking hard core in a porn movie

OR

Your wife in a porn movie getting fucked by Mr big and sucking on a dick that's bigger than yours

WOULD YOU RATHER?

Get fucked by a zombie and then become one

OR

Fuck a zombie and not become one

WOULD YOU RATHER?

Give up your VIP Passes to your favorite band

OR

Get the power to read every mind on the planet

WOULD YOU RATHER?

Gentle juicy blowjob on your parents bed from the wife

OR

Fuck the babysitter gaping anal ass on the wife's bed

Seductive mum shows her stepson how to fuck

WOULD YOU RATHER?

Be the seductive mum

OR

Stepson who learn how to fuck

WOULD YOU RATHER?

Get a rimjob from two tongues at the same time

OR

Rough deep-throat and face fucked

There you have it, the extreme

WOULD YOU RATHER?

Game book for great fun and gross scenarios

We thrive on your reviews.

so if you liked this book and had some extreme fun,

please in your own time come and give us a review of your best bits.

You never know we may feature you in the next one

Made in the USA
Monee, IL
02 July 2020

35710261R00056